# THE TEEN'S MUSICAL THEATRE COLLECTION

## YOUNG WOMEN'S EDITION

Compiled by Louise Lerch

## HAL•LEONARD®
### CORPORATION

7777 W. BLUEMOUND RD. P.O. BOX 13819 MILWAUKEE, WI 53213

Visit Hal Leonard Online at
**www.halleonard.com**

# CONTENTS

## YOUNG WOMEN'S EDITION • NOTES ON THE SONGS

**Beauty and the Beast** from *Beauty and the Beast* (1991, film; 1994, Broadway). This familiar song is performed by the character of Mrs. Potts, and it refers to the overall story of Belle who sees past the Beast's rough persona and learns to love him. (He's a prince, of course.)

**Belle (Reprise)** from *Beauty and the Beast* (1991, film; 1994, Broadway). Belle, a bookish young ingenue, is enamored with Gaston. She fantasizes about who he really is and what their relationship will be. (She later finds out that he is a jerk.)

**Diamonds Are a Girl's Best Friend** from *Gentlemen Prefer Blondes* (1949, Broadway). Set in the 1920s, a good-time, material-girl flapper sings of what she perceives to be a girl's best friend.

**Feed the Birds** from *Mary Poppins* (1964, film). Mary describes to the children the sentimental story of a tenderhearted, old woman in London who takes care of the birds of the city.

**God Help the Outcasts** from *The Hunchback of Notre Dame* (1996, film). Esmerelda is in a church and prays for justice for her people, the outcast gypsies.

**Honey Bun** from *South Pacific* (1949, Broadway). Ensign Nellie Forbush is on an island in the South Pacific during World War II. During a lighthearted moment clowning around with sailors, she performs this vaudeville number to the delight of the listeners.

**I Could Have Danced All Night** from *My Fair Lady* (1956, Broadway). Eliza Doolittle has been taken in by Professor Henry Higgins in order to teach her proper English and raise her social status. She has slaved away for weeks at his phonetic exercises and finally, late one evening for the first time, speaks proper English. Higgins dances with her in delight. She goes to her bedroom and realizes she is in love with him.

**I Enjoy Being a Girl** from *Flower Drum Song* (1958, Broadway). Linda Low is a Chinese American teenager in San Francisco, and in this song, we hear just how American she has become in contrast to her immigrant Chinese parents.

**I Got the Sun in the Morning** from *Annie Get Your Gun* (1946, Broadway). Annie is a sharpshooter in Buffalo Bill's Wild West Show. The show has gone bankrupt and the only way to salvage the show is for Annie to sell her sharpshooting medals. Even though the sacrifice will be hard for Annie, she takes comfort in this song's philosophy.

**I Have Confidence** from *The Sound of Music* (1965, film). Maria von Trapp leaves the safety of the convent to become governess of seven children. She is terrified and uses this song to bolster her courage. This song was not in the Broadway show and was added to the movie version.

**I'll Know** from *Guys and Dolls* (1950, Broadway). Sarah Brown, a Salvation Army worker in New York City, meets a charming gambler and tells him of her ideal mate that she is yet to meet.

**If Momma Was Married** (duet) from *Gypsy* (1959, Broadway). Momma Rose has taken her children on the road in a vaudeville act. Sisters Louise and June wish that their mother would get married again so that they could have a more normal life.

**In My Own Little Corner** from *Cinderella* (1957, television). Cinderella has been abused by her stepmother and stepsisters. She finds her own corner of the kitchen, which is her only refuge, and escapes into her imagination.

**It's a Most Unusual Day** from *A Date with Judy* (1948, film). Not much plot is needed to understand this song. A group of teenagers perform a show for the community and this happy song is part of the act.

**Just You Wait** from *My Fair Lady* (1956, Broadway). Eliza Doolittle, a cockney girl, has been taken in by Henry Higgins. He is driving her crazy with language exercises. At this moment, she hates him and dreams of his demise.

**Many a New Day** from *Oklahoma!* (1943, Broadway). Laurey is a farm girl in Oklahoma. Surrounded by her girlfriends, she playfully claims that no man will get her.

**Memory** from *Cats* (1981, London; 1982, Broadway). This show is based on poems by T.S. Eliot. Grizabella, the glamorous cat "with a past," sings this hopeful ballad at the end of the show.

**Much More** from *The Fantasticks* (1960, Off-Broadway). Luisa is a typical theatre ingenue, and in this song, we meet her beguiling character.

**My Favorite Things** from *The Sound of Music* (1959, Broadway). In the Broadway show, this song is sung by the Mother Abbess and Maria. The Reverend Mother is trying to cheer up the young novice. In the movie, the song has a completely different context. Maria comforts the children in a thunderstorm.

**On My Own** from *Les Misérables* (1980, Paris; 1985, London; 1987, Broadway). Eponine, a street urchin, is in love with Marius. The relationship is hopeless, and she can only dream of a life with him.

**Once Upon a Dream** from *Sleeping Beauty* (1959, film). Sleeping Beauty is out in the forest among her woodland friends. Prince Phillip discovers her there and they dance this enchanting waltz.

**Out of My Dreams** from *Oklahoma!* (1943, Broadway). Laurey, a farm girl from Oklahoma, has fallen in love for the first time. Of course, twenty minutes earlier, she had told everyone that it would be a long time before a man ever got her. But hey, that's musical comedy.

**People Will Say We're in Love** from *Oklahoma!* (1943, Broadway). Laurey and Curly sing this charming love duet before they have begun courting.

**The Simple Joys of Maidenhood** from *Camelot* (1960, Broadway). Guenevere is on her way to Camelot to marry King Arthur. She is panicked at the thought of marrying a man she has never met. She feels she is too young to marry and longs for the "simple" joys that any legendary, medieval princess should expect.

**Sisters** (duet) from *White Christmas* (1954, film). This fun-loving number is performed in a revue as a "show within a show" in the movie. It should be sung as a duet.

**Sixteen Going on Seventeen** from *The Sound of Music* (1959, film). Liesl has taken a liking to Rolf, one year her senior.

**Stepsisters' Lament** from *Cinderella* (1957, television). Cinderella's wicked stepsisters, Portia and Joy, are insanely jealous of Cinderella's success with the prince at the ball.

**There Are Worse Things I Could Do** from *Grease* (1972, Broadway). When Betty Rizzo, a promiscuous teenager, becomes pregnant with an illegitimate baby, she sings this song to defend her way of life.

**Think of Me** from *The Phantom of the Opera* (1986, London; 1988, Broadway). Christine is a chorus girl at the Opéra Populaire in Paris. The prima donna, Carlotta, has refused to perform. Christine sings "Think of Me" as an audition for the impresario.

**Till There Was You** from *The Music Man* (1957, Broadway). Marian Paroo is the librarian in River City, Iowa in 1912. She has tried to resist the charms of Harold Hill, a traveling "music man" and con artist. At the end of the show, Marian and Harold declare their true feelings for each other.

**Unexpected Song** from *Song & Dance* (1981, London; 1985 Broadway). Emma is an English girl living in New York. After many failed relationships, she has finally found the right man for her, even after she had given up hope of ever finding him.

**Wouldn't It Be Loverly** from *My Fair Lady* (1956, Broadway). Eliza Doolittle is a cockney girl who sells flowers in Covent Garden in London. At the top of the show, early in the morning before daybreak, she sings this song with one of her fellow workers about a more comfortable life.

# Beauty and the Beast

### from Walt Disney's BEAUTY AND THE BEAST

Lyrics by HOWARD ASHMAN
Music by ALAN MENKEN

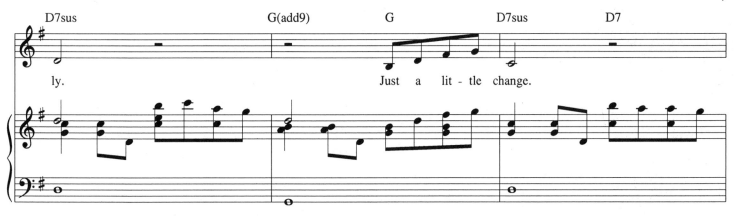

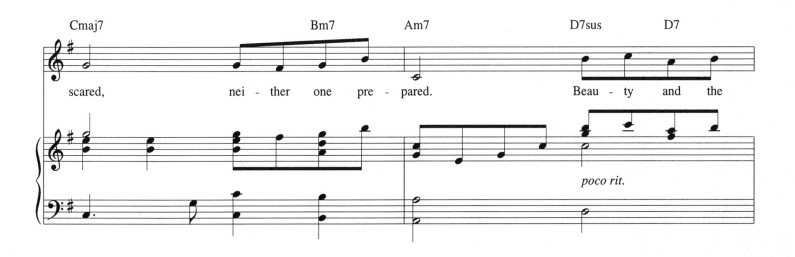

strange, find - ing you can change, learn - ing you were wrong.

Cer - tain as the sun ris - ing in the

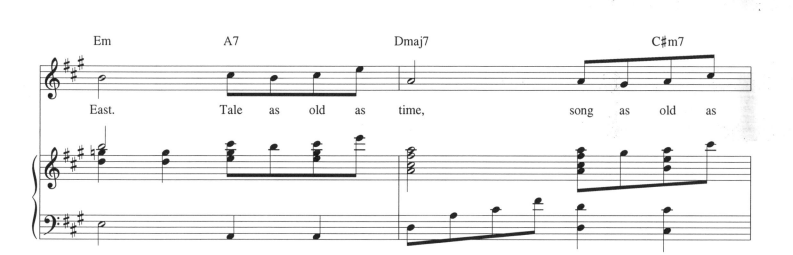

East. Tale as old as time, song as old as

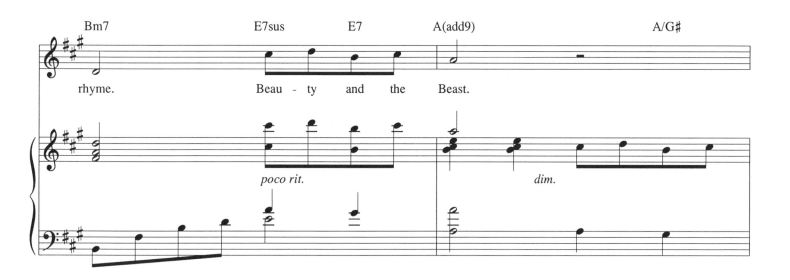

rhyme. Beau - ty and the Beast.

*poco rit.*

*dim.*

Tale as old as time, song as old as rhyme. Beau - ty and the Beast.

# Belle
## (Reprise)
### from Walt Disney's BEAUTY AND THE BEAST

Lyrics by HOWARD ASHMAN
Music by ALAN MENKEN

G/B G Eb F/Eb Eb F/Eb Eb F/Eb
wife." No, sir. Not me! I guar - an -
Bb/D Gm A7 Dsus7 D7
tee it! I want much more than this pro - vin - cial
F/G
life.
cresc.
Broadening
G7 F/G
f
cresc.
8va

# Diamonds Are a Girl's Best Friend

from GENTLEMEN PREFER BLONDES

Words by LEO ROBIN
Music by JULE STYNE

# I Could Have Danced All Night

**from MY FAIR LADY**

Words by ALAN JAY LERNER
Music by FREDERICK LOEWE

18

# Feed the Birds
## from Walt Disney's MARY POPPINS

Words and Music by RICHARD M. SHERMAN
and ROBERT B. SHERMAN

Come feed the lit-tle birds, show them you care And you'll be

glad if you do;_____ Their young ones are hun-gry, their

nests are so bare; All it takes is tup-pence from you._____

CHORUS

Feed _____ the birds, tup-pence _____ a bag, Tup-pence, ___

# God Help the Outcasts

## from Walt Disney's THE HUNCHBACK OF NOTRE DAME

Music by ALAN MENKEN
Lyrics by STEPHEN SCHWARTZ

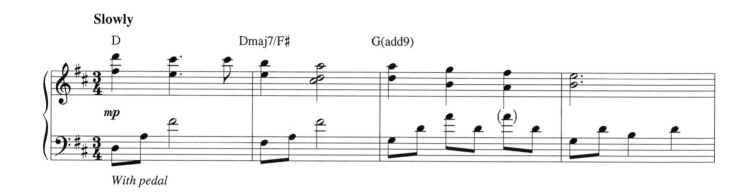

lis - ten to a hum - ble prayer. They tell me I am just an

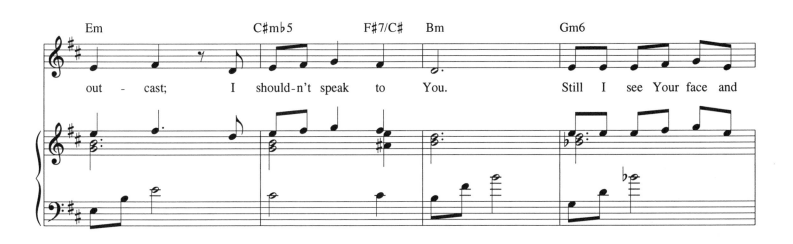

out - cast; I should-n't speak to You. Still I see Your face and

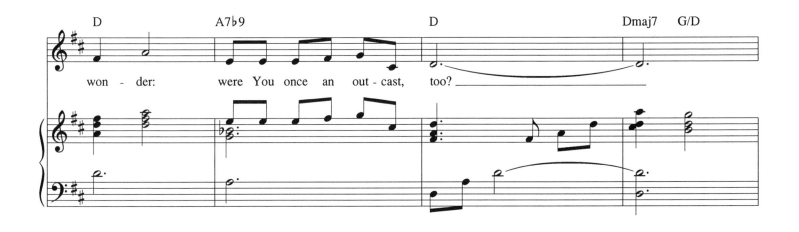

won - der: were You once an out - cast, too? _____

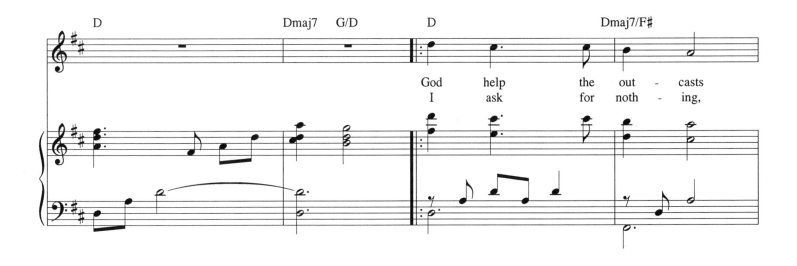

God help the out - casts
I ask for noth - ing,

# Honey Bun

## from SOUTH PACIFIC

Lyrics by OSCAR HAMMERSTEIN II
Music by RICHARD RODGERS

bun! _____ A bun! (Be-lieve me, Son-ny!) She's a

cook-ie who can cook you till ___ you're done, (Ain't be - in' fun-ny)

Son - ny, put your mon-ey on my Hon - ey -

bun! _____

# I Enjoy Being a Girl

## from FLOWER DRUM SONG

Lyrics by OSCAR HAMMERSTEIN II
Music by RICHARD RODGERS

# I Got the Sun in the Morning

### from the Stage Production ANNIE GET YOUR GUN

Words and Music by
IRVING BERLIN

**F7**  **Bb**  **F/A**

press my thanks. _ I got the sun in the morn-ing and the

**Gm7**  **F6**  **Bb**  **F**

moon at night. _____

**Gm7**  **F6**  **F7**  **Bb**  **F/A**  **Abdim**  **Gm7**

And with the sun in the morn-ing and the moon in the eve-ning, I'm _

**C7b9**  **F6**  | **1**  **C7**  | **2**  **Gb7**  **F**

all right. _                                      _

# I'll Know
## from GUYS AND DOLLS

Tune Uke
A D F♯ B

By FRANK LOESSER

* Symbols for Guitar, Diagrams for Ukulele.

# I Have Confidence

## from THE SOUND OF MUSIC

Lyrics and Music by
RICHARD RODGERS

1. I have con-fi-dence in sun-shine.____
2. Let them bring on an-y prob-lems.____

I have con-fi-dence in rain.____
I'll do bet-ter than my best.____

# If Momma Was Married

### from GYPSY

Words by STEPHEN SONDHEIM
Music by JULE STYNE

LOUISE: mar - ried. _____ Mom -

JUNE: ma, get out your white dress! You've done it be - fore With - out much suc -

BOTH: cess. Mom - - - - ma, God

speed and God bless, We're not keep - ing score. What's one more or less?

# In My Own Little Corner
## from CINDERELLA

Lyrics by OSCAR HAMMERSTEIN II
Music by RICHARD RODGERS

# It's a Most Unusual Day
## from A DATE WITH JUDY

Words by HAROLD ADAMSON
Music by JIMMY McHUGH

# Just You Wait
### from MY FAIR LADY

Words by ALAN JAY LERNER
Music by FREDERICK LOEWE

wait! _____ Just you wait, 'en - ry 'ig - gins, till you're

sick, _____ And you scream to fetch a doc - tor doub - le -

quick! _____ I'll be off a sec - ond la - ter, And go

straight to the the - a - tre! Oh, ho ho, 'en - ry 'ig - gins, just you wait.

Oooooooh, 'en - ry 'ig - gins! Just you

wait un - til we're swim-min' in the sea!

Oooooooh, 'en - ry 'ig - gins And you

get a cramp a lit - tle ways from me! When you

yell you're gon-na drown, I'll get dressed and go to town! Oh, ho,

ho, 'en-ry 'ig-gins! Oh, ho, ho, 'en-ry 'ig-gins!

Just you wait! One ___

day I'll be fam-ous! I'll be pro-per and prim! Go to

Saint James so oft - en I will call it Saint Jim. One _

eve - ning the King will say, "Oh, Li - za, old thing, I

want _ all of Eng - land your prai - ses to sing. Next

week, on the twen - ti - eth of May, I pro-

all I want is 'en-ry 'ig-gins 'ead!"

*poco rit.*

*f a tempo*

**Poco più mosso**

"Done," says the King, "with a stroke.

*mf*

Guard, run and bring— in the bloke!"    Then they'll

*ff*    *mf*

**Allegro marziale**

march you, 'en-ry 'ig-gins, to the wall;    And the

king will tell me: "Li - za, sound the call."_____ As they

raise their ri - fles high - er, I'll shout: "Rea - dy! Aim! Fire!" Oh, ho,

(muffled Dr.)

ho! 'en - ry 'ig - gins! Down you'll go! 'en - ry 'ig - gins!

Just you wait!

# Many a New Day
## from OKLAHOMA!

Lyrics by OSCAR HAMMERSTEIN II
Music by RICHARD RODGERS

Why should a wom-an who is health-y and strong, blub-ber like a ba-by if her man goes a-way? A-weep-in' and a-wail-in' how he done her wrong, that's one thing you'll nev-er hear me say! Nev-er gon-na think that the

# Much More
## from THE FANTASTICKS

Words by TOM JONES
Music by HARVEY SCHMIDT

Moderato

Refrain - con moto

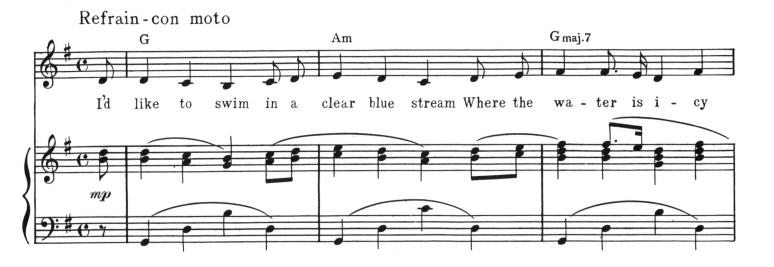

I'd like to swim in a clear blue stream Where the wa - ter is i - cy

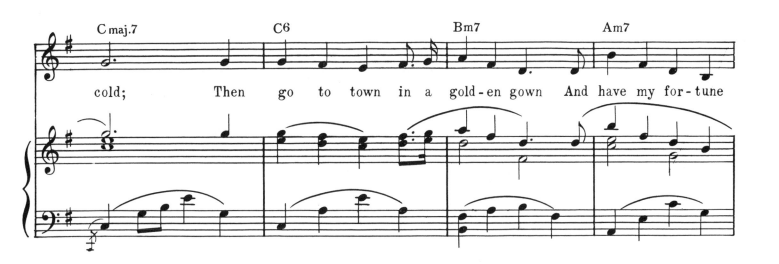

cold; Then go to town in a gold - en gown And have my for - tune

# Memory
## from CATS

Music by ANDREW LLOYD WEBBER
Text by TREVOR NUNN after T.S. ELIOT

# My Favorite Things
### from THE SOUND OF MUSIC

Lyrics by OSCAR HAMMERSTEIN II
Music by RICHARD RODGERS

# On My Own

## from LES MISÉRABLES

Music by CLAUDE-MICHEL SCHONBERG
Lyrics by ALAIN BOUBLIL, HERBERT KRETZMER, JOHN CAIRD,
TREVOR NUNN and JEAN-MARC NATEL

# People Will Say We're in Love

## from OKLAHOMA!

Lyrics by OSCAR HAMMERSTEIN II
Music by RICHARD RODGERS

# Once Upon a Dream

from Walt Disney's SLEEPING BEAUTY

Words and Music by SAMMY FAIN and JACK LAWRENCE
Adapted from a Theme by TCHAIKOVSKY

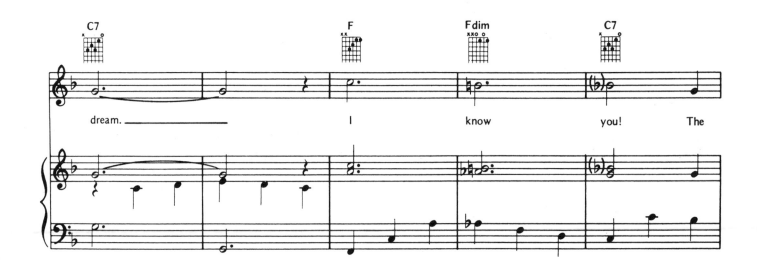

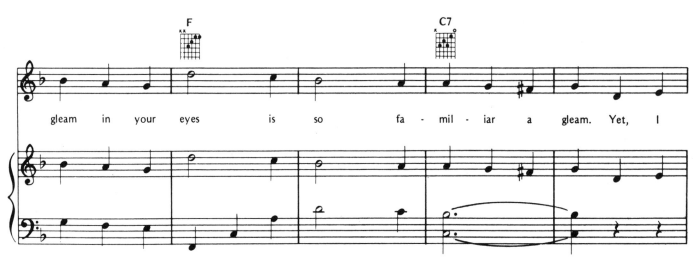

# Out of My Dreams
## from OKLAHOMA!

Lyrics by OSCAR HAMMERSTEIN II
Music by RICHARD RODGERS

# Part of Your World
## from Walt Disney's THE LITTLE MERMAID

Lyrics by HOWARD ASHMAN
Music by ALAN MENKEN

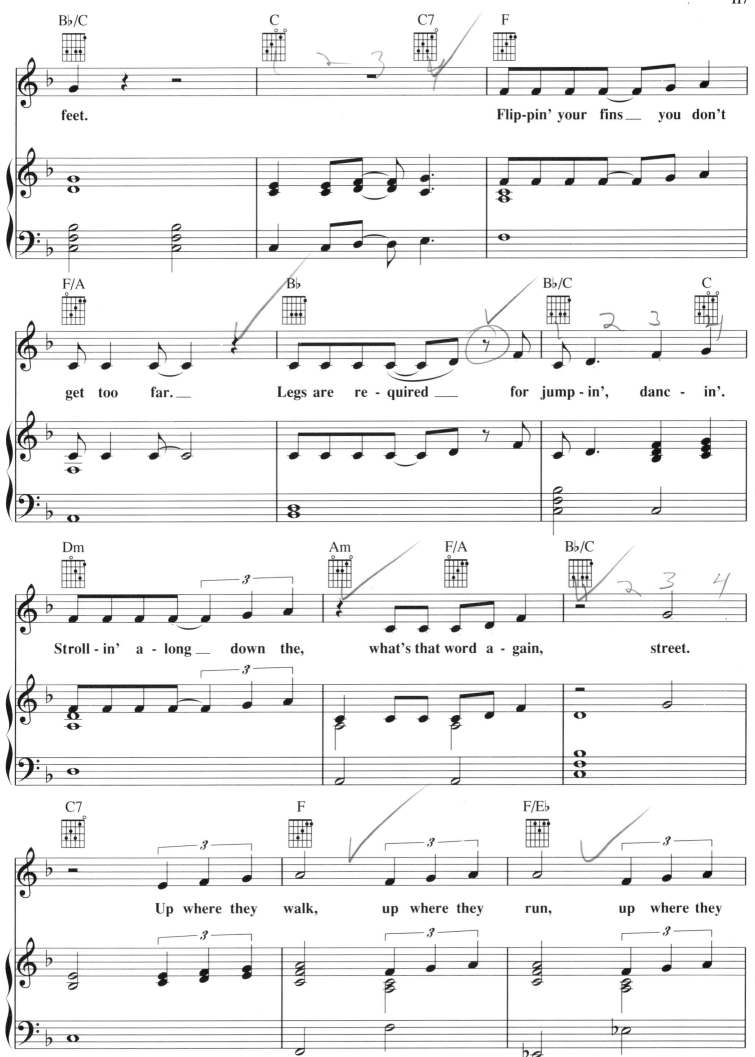

# The Simple Joys of Maidenhood
## from CAMELOT

Words by ALAN JAY LERNER
Music by FREDERICK LOEWE

# Sisters
## from WHITE CHRISTMAS

Words and Music by
IRVING BERLIN

Sis - ters,     sis - ters,
(Male) Broth - ers,     broth - ers,

there were nev - er such de - vot - ed sis - ters.     Nev - er had to have a chap - er-
there were nev - er such de - vot - ed broth - ers.     When there comes a glam - our girl who's

# Sixteen Going on Seventeen

### from THE SOUND OF MUSIC

Lyrics by OSCAR HAMMERSTEIN II
Music by RICHARD RODGERS

# Stepsisters' Lament

### from CINDERELLA

Lyrics by OSCAR HAMMERSTEIN II
Music by RICHARD RODGERS

# There are Worse Things I Could Do

## from GREASE

Lyric and Music by
WARREN CASEY and JIM JACOBS

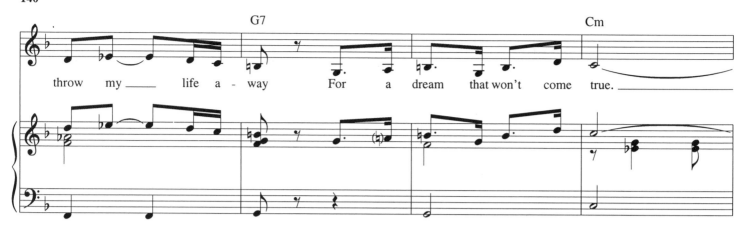

throw my _____ life a - way For a dream that won't come true. _____

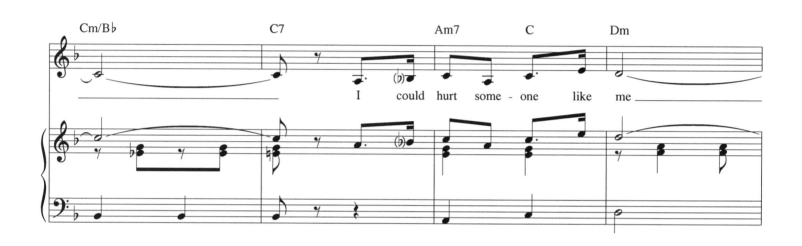

_____ I could hurt some - one like me _____

_____ Out of spite or _____ jeal - ous - y. _____

_____ I don't steal and _____ I don't lie but _____ I can

# Think of Me
## from THE PHANTOM OF THE OPERA

Music by ANDREW LLOYD WEBBER
Lyrics by CHARLES HART
Additional Lyrics by RICHARD STILGOE

**Allegretto**

CHRISTINE

Think of me,

think of me fond - ly    when we've said good - bye.    Re - mem - ber me

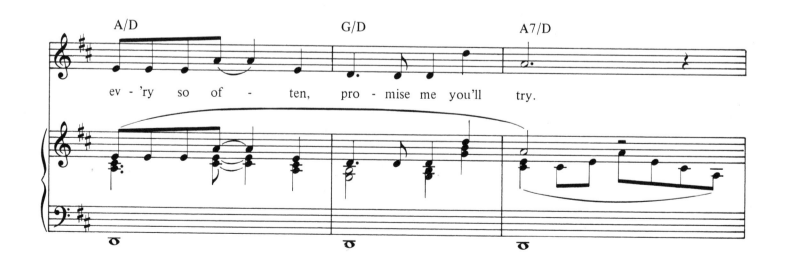

ev - 'ry so of - ten,    pro - mise me you'll    try.

And though it's clear,__ though it was al - ways clear__ that this was

nev - er meant to be, if you hap-pen to re - mem - ber,

stop and think of me. Think of Au - gust when the

trees were green; don't think a - bout the way things

Raoul's section may be an instrumental interlude.

# Till There Was You

### from Meredith Willson's THE MUSIC MAN

By MEREDITH WILLSON

# Unexpected Song
## from SONG & DANCE

Music by ANDREW LLOYD WEBBER
Lyrics by DON BLACK

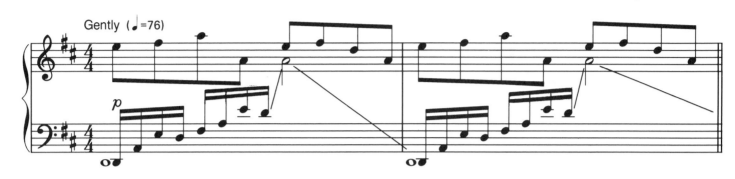

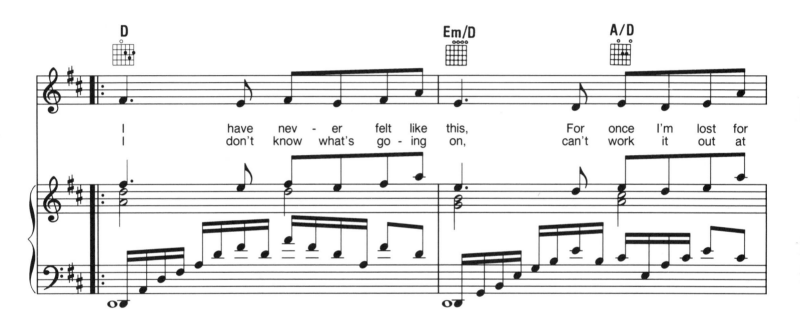

I
have nev-er felt like this,     For once I'm lost for
I
don't know what's go-ing on,     can't work it out at

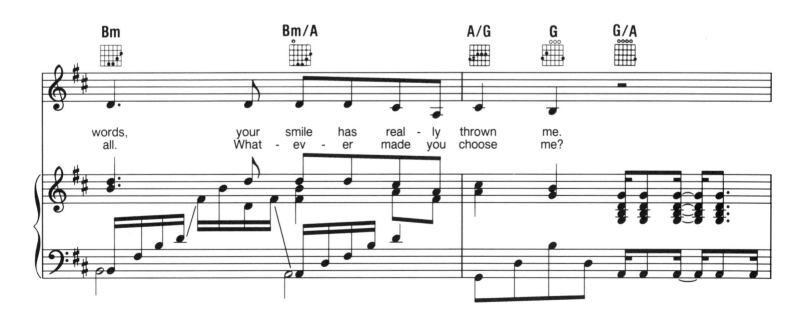

words,              your smile has real-ly thrown me.
all.     What-ev-er made you choose me?

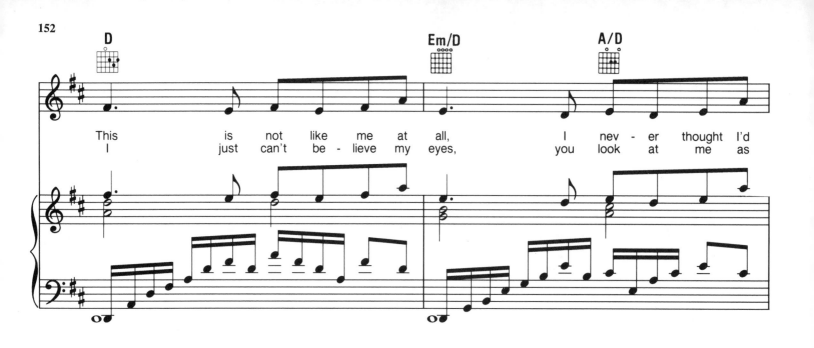

This is not like me at all,  I nev-er thought I'd
I just can't be-lieve my eyes,  you look at me as

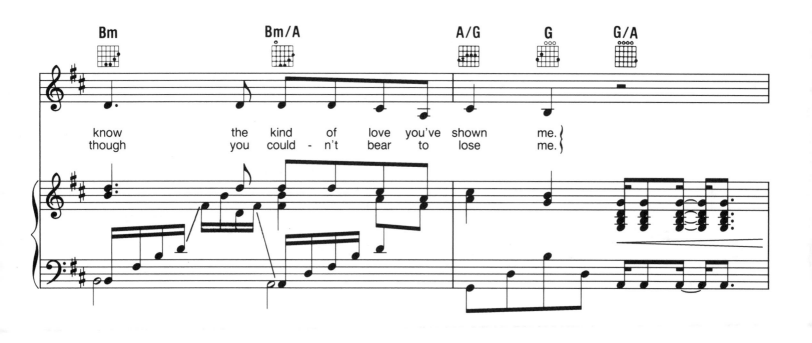

know the kind of love you've shown me.
though you could-n't bear to lose me.

Now no mat-ter where I am, no mat-ter what I do, I see your face ap-

thrown me. This is not like me at all, I nev-er thought I'd

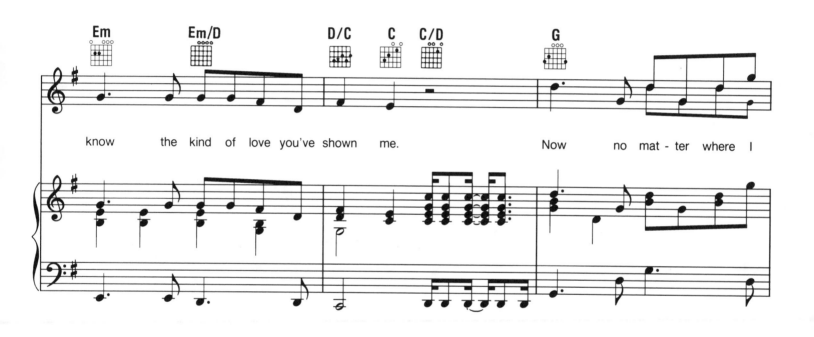

know the kind of love you've shown me. Now no mat-ter where I

am, no mat-ter what I do, I see your face ap-pear-ing like an un-ex-pect-ed

song, an un-ex-pect-ed song that on-ly we are hear - ing.

Like an un-ex-pect-ed song, an un-ex-pect-ed song that on-ly we are

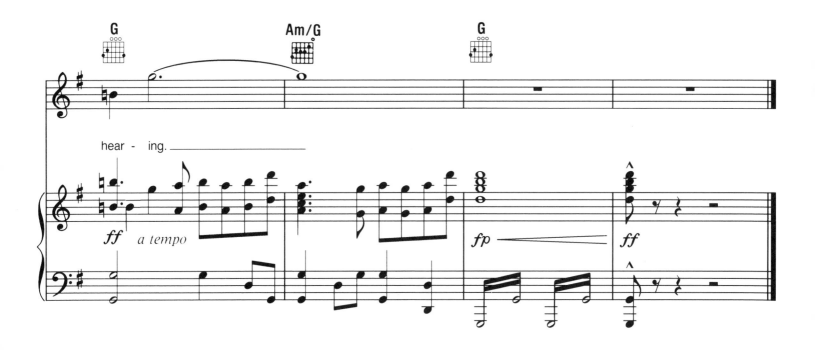

hear - ing.

# Wouldn't It Be Loverly
## from MY FAIR LADY

Words by ALAN JAY LERNER
Music by FREDERICK LOEWE

# MUSICAL THEATRE COLLECTIONS
## FROM HAL LEONARD

### BROADWAY BELTER'S SONGBOOK

A great new collection for women singers. All the songs have been chosen especially for this type of voice, and the ranges and keys have been carefully selected. 30 songs, including: Broadway Baby • The Lady Is A Tramp • Everything's Coming Up Roses • I'd Give My Life To You (*Miss Saigon*) • Cabaret. 176 pages.
_____ 00311608 ................................. $16.95

### THE SINGER'S MUSICAL THEATRE ANTHOLOGY

The most comprehensive collection of Broadway selections ever organized specifically for the singer. Each of the five volumes contains important songs chosen because of their appropriateness to that particular voice type. All selections are in their authentic form, excerpted from the original vocal scores. The songs in *The Singer's Musical Theatre Anthology*, written by such noted composers as Kurt Weill, Richard Rodgers, Stephen Sondheim, and Jerome Kern, are vocal masterpieces ideal for the auditioning, practicing or performing vocalist.

#### Soprano
46 songs, including: Where Or When • If I Loved You • Goodnight, My Someone • Smoke Gets In Your Eyes • Barbara Song • and many more.
_____ 00361071 ................................. $19.95

#### Mezzo-Soprano/Alto
40 songs, including: My Funny Valentine • I Love Paris • Don't Cry For Me Argentina • Losing My Mind • Send In The Clowns • and many more.
_____ 00361072 ................................. $19.95

#### Tenor
42 songs, including: Stranger In Paradise • On The Street Where You Live • Younger Than Springtime • Lonely House • Not While I'm Around • and more.
_____ 00361073 ................................. $19.95

#### Baritone/Bass
37 songs, including: If Ever I Would Leave You • September Song • The Impossible Dream • Ol' Man River • Some Enchanted Evening • and more.
_____ 00361074 ................................. $19.95

#### Duets
21 songs, including: Too Many Mornings • We Kiss In A Shadow • People Will Say We're In Love • Bess You Is My Woman • Make Believe • more.
_____ 00361075 ................................. $16.95

### THE SINGER'S MUSICAL THEATRE ANTHOLOGY VOL. 2

More great theatre songs for singers in a continuation of this highly successful and important series, once again compiled and edited by Richard Walters. As is the case with the first volume, these collections are as valuable to the classical singer as they are to the popular and theatre performer.

#### Soprano, Volume 2
42 songs, including: All Through The Night • And This Is My Beloved • Vilia • If I Were A Bell • Think Of Me.
_____ 00747066 ................................. $19.95

#### Mezzo-Soprano/Alto, Volume 2
44 songs, including: If He Walked Into My Life • The Party's Over • Johnny One Note • Adalaide's Lament • I Hate Men • I Dreamed A Dream.
_____ 00747031 ................................. $19.95

#### Tenor, Volume 2
46 songs, including: Miracle Of Miracles • Sit Down, You're Rockin' The Boat • Giants In The Sky • Bring Him Home • Music Of The Night.
_____ 00747032 ................................. $19.95

#### Baritone/Bass, Volume 2
44 songs, including: Guido's Song from *Nine* • Bye, Bye Baby • I Won't Send Roses • The Surrey With The Fringe On Top • Once In Love With Amy.
_____ 00747033 ................................. $19.95

### THE ACTOR'S SONGBOOK

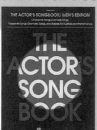

A wonderfully diverse collection of comedy songs, character songs, Vaudeville numbers, dramatic songs, and ballads for the actor who sings. A perfect resource to use for finding an audition song or specialty number. In two editions, one for women, and one for men, with a completely different selection of songs chosen for each edition. Over 50 songs in each book. Women's edition titles include: The Ladies Who Lunch • Cla-wence (Don't Tweat Me So Wough) • Cry Me A River • Shy • The Man That Got Away, and many more. Men's edition includes: Buddy's Blues (from *Follies*) • Doing The Reactionary • How to Handle A Woman • I'm Calm • Reviewing The Situation, many more.
_____ 00747035 Women's Edition ...................... $19.95
_____ 00747034 Men's Edition ......................... $19.95

FOR MORE INFORMATION, SEE YOUR LOCAL MUSIC DEALER, OR WRITE TO:

# HAL•LEONARD®
## CORPORATION
7777 W. BLUEMOUND RD. P.O. BOX 13819 MILWAUKEE, WI 53213

Prices, contents and availability subject to change without notice.

### KIDS' BROADWAY SONGBOOK

An unprecedented collection of songs that were originally performed by children on the Broadway stage. A terrific and much needed publication for the thousands of children studying voice. Includes 16 songs for boys and girls: Gary, Indiana (*The Music Man*) • Castle On A Cloud (*Les Miserables*) • Where Is Love? (*Oliver!*) • Tomorrow (*Annie*) • and more.
_____ 00311609 ................................. $9.95

### MUSICAL THEATRE CLASSICS

A fantastic series featuring the best songs from Broadway classics. Collections are organized by voice type and each book includes recorded piano accompaniments on CD – ideal for practicing. Compiled by Richard Walters, Sue Malmberg, pianist.

#### Soprano, Volume 1
13 songs, including: Climb Ev'ry Mountain • Falling In Love With Love • Hello, Young Lovers • Smoke Gets In Your Eyes • Wishing You Were Somehow Here Again.
_____ 00740036 ................................. $19.95

#### Soprano, Volume 2
13 more favorites, including: Can't Help Lovin' Dat Man • I Could Have Danced All Night • Show Me • Think Of Me • Till There Was You.
_____ 00740037 ................................. $19.95

#### Mezzo-Soprano/Alto, Volume 1
11 songs, including: Don't Cry For Me Argentina • I Dreamed A Dream • The Lady Is A Tramp • People • and more.
_____ 00740038 ................................. $19.95

#### Mezzo-Soprano/Alto, Volume 2
11 songs, including: Glad To Be Unhappy • Just You Wait • Memory • My Funny Valentine • On My Own • and more.
_____ 00740039 ................................. $19.95

#### Tenor
11 songs, including: All I Need Is A Girl • If You Could See Her • The Music Of The Night • On The Street Where You Live • Younger Than Springtime • and more.
_____ 00740040 ................................. $19.95

#### Baritone/Bass
11 classics, including: If Ever I Would Leave You • If I Loved You • Oh, What A Beautiful Mornin' • Ol' Man River • Try To Remember • and more.
_____ 00740041 ................................. $19.95